MORE

J Golden
Kimball
Stories

by

James Kimball

J. Golden Kimball

MORE
J. Golden
Kimball
STORIES

James Kimball

illustrations by
Pat Bagley

More J. Golden Kimball Stories
copyright 2002 White Horse Books
all rights reserved
Printed in the United States

First Edition

9 8 7 6 5 4 3 2 1

library of congress lccn

ISBN 1-56684-662-5

cover art and design Pat Bagley

editors Linda Bult
and Marti Esplin

transcribed from audio
Julie DeHerrera

Acknowledgments

I have long been a fan of Pat Bagley's gentle and wry humor. I cannot begin my day without first examining his witty take on the social and political issues so brilliantly crafted in his political cartoons.

This gift he has adds so very much to the enjoyment of this book. I wish to thank Pat for suggesting we jointly create now two volumes of J. Golden's stories.

I should like to also express my appreciation to Linda Bult, my editor for this book. She guided this project with a steady hand from its inception several months ago. Her calm and pleasant nature made the project and the deadlines all very manageable for me.

Also thanks to Julie DeHerrera for transcribing these stories from tape and to Marty Esplin for copy editing.

I feel very indebted to Elizabeth Searles and all the other gifted and likable people at KUED who brought the life and humor of Uncle Golden to the attention of so very many.

Introduction

J. Golden Kimball died in 1933 in a car accident in Nevada—the only General Authority in modern times to perish by means of an accident. Believe it or not, some people attach ominous significance to this fact: "See what happens when you swear!"

So what does happen to a soul that swears like a cowboy, has a lightning-quick wit, and loves the Gospel with all his heart?

He apparently gets to poke self-important people with a sharp stick all of his life until the fates catch up with him at age eighty-five.

And then he gets to live forever.

J. Golden Kimball's immortality comes from these stories that refuse to fade from popular memory. In fact, far from fading, Golden's exploits seem to multiply: Nice trick for a man seven decades dead.

These are stories that have been passed down around campfires, dinner tables, and in sacrament meetings for almost a century. Many are classics that continue to tickle the under arms of our self-importance no matter how many times we hear them.

Some are stories that are on the verge of being taken to the grave and slipping away forever. They are literally rescued at the last moment by a neice, nephew, or grandchild who bothers to rummage around in an aged relative's accumulated lifetime of memories by asking, "Did you ever know J. Golden Kimball?"

Some stories attributed to Golden are pure folklore. They never occured. Even when he was alive "J. Golden Kimball" tales circulated that were news to him. On being informed of another story in which he played the leading role, Golden responded that "everything these days is either blamed on me or Mae West!"

But the fact that we *want* these stories to be true reveals much about us and shouldn't diminish the pleasure we take from them. We want permission to say "damn" and "hell" once in a while, even if it means hiding under the coattails of a long dead General Authority to make it okay.

After *J. Golden Kimball Stories* was published in 1999, new stories have poured in from wonderful people who discovered another forgotten Golden treasure lying around in someone's dusty attic. Keep them coming! You might be surprised what turns up by simply asking an older brother or sister in the ward, "Do you remember J. Golden Kimball?"

The Publisher

Author's Note

J. Golden Kimball continues to remain a legendary figure both in and outside the Mormon Culture. He has been transformed by those who remember him from a complex entity that was a man into a uni-dimensional entity that is a true American folk hero.

Indeed, various authors have compiled so much information about his life as to, thus far, produce two biographies, three books quoting his wit and wisdom, several published articles in historical and literary journals, two award-winning KUED videos, over two hundred of my "Remembering Uncle Golden" performances across the country, and next summer, a full-length Hollywood film.

I have often been asked what it is about his character and wit that has made him so enduring to so many people. In my efforts to understand the emotional and spiritual core of this good man, I have concluded that he was in possession of an unvarnished spontaneity, one seldom observed, particularly in a Mormon church setting.

A certain amount of order is needed to avoid chaos, but an occasional reprieve does not hurt. Uncle Golden's perceptive talent for knowing when and where to add a little spice to the monotony of order always provided a much needed breath of fresh air.

He was a man of distinctive free will. His unusual type of humor was self-deprecating, unstudied, and completely devoid of pretense.

Here, then, was a common man contending with himself, yet in possession of an unusual ability to acknowledge his struggle and describe it with both wit and insight.

I believe people felt a oneness with such a rare man and continued to love him all the more for it.

James Kimball
August 2002

Those that I like and admire I can find
no common denominator. But those that
I love, I can. They all make me laugh.

—W. H. Auden

Bear Lake Stories

Leap of Faith

When Heber C. Kimball died, there was a little money in the will left to Golden's mother, Christeen Golden Kimball. She took that money and with her daughter, Mary Margaret, and two sons, Golden and Elias, bought some ground in the Bear Lake area where the family started a ranching-farming operation.

It was a hard scrabble existence. It was tough. It was cold. But eventually they made a success of it.

Up to this point in his life, Golden had shown no interest in the Church. He was running with a wild bunch of swearin'-gamblin'-tobacco-chewin'-no-good-rough-neck cowboys.

This worried and concerned his mother.

She often hinted that he should go on a mission. Golden was a good son and didn't like disappointing his mother, but he couldn't work up an interest in God when God had apparently shown so little interest in him. So he continued with his wild friends when the ranch didn't need his attention.

In his later years, he would tell of the experience that changed his life forever.

He was thirty years old. In the fall they brought in all the cows and the one bull from the mountains around Bear Lake where the cattle had their summer range. The Kimballs rounded up all the cows, but they couldn't find the bull. Golden and his brother, Elias, rode through the mountains and canyons trying to find the prodigal beast.

A neighbor told them they thought they had seen the bull on a nearby plateau. There was only one trail to the top, so if the bull happened to be there, it wouldn't be able to slip past them. They rode up to look at the spot. Sure enough, there he was. The bull had been enjoying his freedom and didn't want anything to do with the two cowboys. He ducked and dodged but couldn't get by the Kimball boys. Finally they had him cornered. Three sides of the plateau dropped off two to three hundred feet. They had their bull.

They broke out their lariats and twirled them over their heads to nab the stubborn animal. They slowly edged him to where he had no room to manuever. The bull knew what was coming. He was going to be lassoed and trotted back to some corral for the winter. He wanted none of that. He had enjoyed himself too much, having free run of the mountains and the canyons and the plateaus.

The bull charged.

15

The horses shied away, but didn't let him pass. Then, strangely enough, the bull turned and ran full speed off the end of the plateau. He fell headlong into the canyon below, killing himself.

Golden and Elias rode to the edge of the plateau and peered down. There was nothing but blood and gore. For some time, Golden looked at the depressing sight of their prize bull splashed all over the rocks. Turning to Elias he said, "That's the way it's going to end for me if I don't change my ways."

At home he told his mother that he would go see President John Taylor in Salt Lake about going on a mission. He'd reform himself and serve God.

That is how Golden began a lifetime of service to the Church. The rough and sometimes crude cowboy would eventually be transformed into a rough and sometimes crude General Authority. But his honest spirituality and wit endeared him to this people in such a way that even seventy years after his death, Latter-day Saints still love hearing J. Golden Kimball stories.

And that's no bull.

Bear With Me

Throughout his life, he used many homey phrases that came from those years. He would often say that his character was much like that of a young colt in a spring pasture. Or he once described how thin he was by saying he was so thin he could get shade out of a barbwire fence.

Those years in the Bear Lake area stayed with Uncle Golden for the rest of his life. I believe they shaped much of his character. He learned how to work very hard. He knew what it was like to be poor.

Fish Story

Uncle Golden always looked forward to an assignment that brought him back to the Bear Lake area. Going back to Randolph to the Stake Tabernacle to speak and renew friendships was almost a vacation.

Feeling at home, Golden would let his hair down (so to speak–Uncle Golden was bald at an early age). Many stories came out of those talks he gave. The following is illustrative of his subtle wit.

He was in the Bear Lake area to speak at conference. He was sitting on the stand along with the stake president, who was new to the job. The stake president was a very hard working and dedicated man who was proud of his stake.

He stood and introduced Golden. He then took the time, as some stake presidents are accustomed to doing, and laid it on pretty thick about what a great stake he had the honor of presiding over. He praised the amazing group of people who made up his stake and rattled off statistics that proved just how outstanding they were. (One often sees this in Church meetings even today.)

This stake president said that his Bear River Stake had some of the most faithful people in the Church: Temple attendance was off the charts, it had one of the highest percentages in the Church in the number of elders sent out on missions, and it boasted more full tithe payers than any other stake of similar size and disposition.

And then he floated a truly remarkable statistic. He claimed that local sacrament meeting attendance—which is always a measure of faithfulness in any stake—was the highest in the entire restored Church: An amazing ninety-five percent regularly turned out.

Golden knew this was wishful thinking on the stake president's part: Too many people are offended each Sunday to consistently come back with any regularity. Ninety-five percent was clearly pie in the sky. But Golden held his tongue.

The stake president finished his litany of sterling accomplishments and gave the floor to my uncle. Golden bellied up to the pulpit and, completely ignoring all the glowing reports of statistical faithfulness, launched into a story.

"Brothers and sisters, I always enjoy coming here and being with you. I was here about a year ago. It was Saturday. I got a call from an old friend over in Rand Valley and he said, 'Let's go fishing, Golden, it's a warm, beautiful summer afternoon, and I got the rods and reels and the bait, and the fish are going to be biting. Why don't you come along?'

"I said, 'I can't do it—I've got to go attend a welfare meeting.' And he said, 'Oh, Golden, you know how boring those welfare meetings are. Go get somebody else to do it. You come fishing with me.' I said, 'I'll see if I can find somebody....

"In five minutes I called him back and said I would go.

"So off we went. We rowed a boat out to the middle of Bear Lake and cast our lines out. It was very pleasant. Very relaxing. Although there was not much in the way of any fish biting.

"But as it became dusk the fish started to bite. We were reeling them in and before we knew it night had fallen. So this brother lit a lantern and put it up front of the boat. We kept fishing until a wind picked up. I said, 'We better get back to shore or we'll get swamped.' We rowed towards the shore, but, sure enough, we got swamped and the boat sank.

"I damn near drowned, brothers and sisters."

The congregation started to fidget, wondering where this story was going. "We made it to shore. And know what? That same brother called me up yesterday to go fishing. I said, 'No, I'm not going with you. You damn near killed me last time!' He said, 'It's a beautiful day. C'mon, Golden, forgive me; I'm sorry about last year. I've got a new boat. It's got a tin bottom. It won't sink.'

"He talked me into it, brothers and sisters. We rowed his new boat out into the lake.

"I was looking down in that green grass you could see down at the bottom. And there, brothers and sisters, much to my amazement, I saw the boat from the previous year! There it was. I said, 'Stop! Look!' It was thirty feet down and we could see that the rods and reels and even the fish were all still in the boat. And there was the lantern in the front of the boat. And, brothers and sisters, that lantern was still lit! Can you believe that? That lantern was still lit!"

Golden's audience was totally befuddled. Here was a General Authority asking them to believe something that clearly couldn't be true. He then asked the stake president to come up to the podium with him. He put his arm around the man and said, "Now tell me, president, do you believe that story about fishing on Bear Lake?"

The uncomfortable brother said, "Well, Brother Kimball, I could have believed it until you got to the last part. A lantern can't remain lit in a boat in the bottom of the lake for one year. That's impossible."

Golden smiled and said, "Listen brother, you take fifteen percent off that sacrament meeting attendance and I'll douse the lantern."

21

Promise Keeper

Here is another Bear Lake story. There was a young man that Golden knew in the valley up there. He was a very enterprising young fellow. He had a team of horses and a wagon. He made a good living hauling things for folks: hay, manure, dirt, lumber, firewood—whatever needed hauling.

Then, unexpectedly, he was called on a mission. Being twenty years old with a thriving business, he was reluctant go.

He stopped by Golden's ranch for counsel. "Should I accept this mission call? I have a good business going here and a promising future. I can get married soon and raise a family. Accepting a mission call at this time would be a real hardship. What should I do, Brother Kimball?"

Golden felt the young man's anguish. Earlier in his life, he too had to leave a going concern to serve the Lord. But he also knew what mattered in the eternal scheme of things. "Listen, brother—you've been called to serve the Lord. I think you should accept the call."

"Sell your horses and your wagon and take that money to support yourself in the mission field. I promise you, brother, that the Lord will bless you when you come back. In a very short time, you shall have a team of horses and a wagon and you'll be back in business again. Everything will be just as it was before because the Lord will take care of you if you do his work."

22

The young brother did exactly as Golden advised. He sold his precious team and wagon. He went on his mission and honorably served the Lord.

When he returned, Utah and the rest of the nation were in the throes of the Great Depression. Despite diligence and hard work, he couldn't pull anything together to provide a living. There was never enough work to earn money for a new team and wagon. He was desperate.

At last he came to see Golden. Seated in the living room of the Kimball home, he spelled out his plight. "Brother Kimball, I did as you advised me and remained faithful. I've served an honorable mission, but I can't seem to put it together. You told me the Lord would provide for me when I returned, but I'm flat broke with no prospects."

Golden said, "Follow me, brother." He led the way into the backyard and out to the corral. There were Golden's team and wagon.

"Here, brother, you take this. This is yours now."

"I can't do that, Brother Kimball! That—that's too much; I couldn't!"

"No, you take it. Don't make me use my priesthood authority on you. Now get started and things will work out. You'll be okay."

The young man jumped up and whooped, hardly believing his

good fortune. He hitched up the horses and went down the road and out of the ranch.

Then Golden's wife, Jennie, came out and saw the departing team. "Golden, what's happening? That looks like our team of horses and wagon. What's that young man doing with it?"

With hands on hips, Golden watched his team disappear in the distance. "Hell, if the Lord won't keep his promises, then I will."

God's Country

According to Golden, the weather in Bear Lake was "one month of late summer and eleven months of dead winter." But he was proud of his little homestead all the same. He had kept it after his mother died and loved to go up there on weekends and holidays.

Once, when President Grant was in the area for a conference, Golden showed him his ranch. He drove President Grant around his farm and showed him the horses, cattle, fence lines, and irrigation canals.

As President Grant left to get in the car to drive back to Salt Lake, he shook Golden's hand and said, "Brother Kimball, you have a wonderful ranch here."

Golden's reply was, "You should have seen it when just God ran it.

President Grant & Golden

"Heber"

These opening episodes drawn from the life of Uncle Golden are stories that he had pretty much kept to himself about the president of the Church, Heber J. Grant. He never called him "President Grant"; he always just called him "Heber."

On special occasions with the family or with close friends, he would occasionally open up and share a few of these intimate remembrances of the man who was president of the Church through most of the time that Golden was a General Authority. (Uncle Golden was one of the Seven Presidents of the Seventies from 1892 to his death in 1938).

Golden once accompanied President Grant to a stake conference in southern Idaho. At that conference, President Grant was delivering his favorite sermon. The theme was "That Which We Persist in Doing Will Lead to Success"—another way of saying practice makes perfect. Those who remember President Grant will no doubt recall that this was a recurring theme in his sermons.

A sermon, by the way, that Golden had heard far too often.

The president began by speaking of his inability to sing as a youth and how it took some time for him to develop this talent through persistence, practice, and lessons. He told the audience, "When I began this task, I couldn't tell one note from another."

Golden, who was seated immediately behind President Grant on the podium, quipped loud enough for everyone on the stand, but not the audience, to hear, "If that had been a bank note, he could have told the difference!"

To the puzzlement of the audience, everyone sitting on the rostrum burst into laughter. President Grant, who was not deaf, pretended not to have heard Golden's retort and ran right on with the remainder of his sermon.

Fear of Flying

During much of President Grant's long tenure as president of the Church, Rudger Clawson was president of the Quorum of the Twelve Apostles. As such, he was next in line to become the Prophet, Seer, and Revelator should President Grant pass away.

Rudger was widely known as a somewhat humorless and rigorous workhorse in the Church. Golden, of course, was a horse of a different color....

Uncle Golden's spontaneous approach to life was deeply trying to Brother Clawson—more so even than it was to President Grant. Golden always contended that Heber was his "best friend in the First Presidency or all of the Quorum of the Twelve." He explained it this way:

"Heber has a great curiosity about airplanes and flying. He is well aware of how dangerous this is, but he still wants to do it. I'm sure that one day he will go out to the airport and get in an airplane and fly up in the air. I personally don't care if he does it or not—he just has to wait till Rudger dies."

He went on to guess that "maybe he hasn't gone flying as a favor to me. I have to admit, I'm in his debt."

Spit and Polish

The Angel Moroni atop the Salt Lake Temple was badly in need of cleaning and extensive repair work. The First Presidency called for bids, but none were submitted by anyone in Utah. It was simply too dangerous.

They inquired of several professional steeplejacks in the East. A gentleman in New York responded. The Church sent him a railway ticket to travel to Salt Lake so he could give a bid after examining the Angel Moroni in person.

Well, this small, wirey, muscular fellow soon arrived. Without wasting any time at all, he put on his work clothes and climbed to the highest spire of the temple to examine the condition of the Angel Moroni and then came down and closeted himself away to tote up the numbers.

31

A few hours later, he presented a bid of several thousand dollars—an enormous amount in those days.

Golden tells what happened next: "Heber asked this steeplejack to come in and see him. Upon arriving he was immediately ushered into Heber's office. Heber introduced himself and then added, 'Sir, this bid is preposterous! How can you ask such an outlandish fee?'

"The little man from New York scratched his beard and said, 'Well, Mr. Grant, you have no idea how dirty that old son of a bitch is!'

"Everything became very quiet. Heber had to sit down for a minute to collect himself. He then called his secretary in and told her to prepare a check for the full amount of the bid.

"I'm the only one he ever told that story to. He said he thought I would understand and approve. And, quite frankly, I do."

Horn Blower

Speaking of the Salt Lake Temple and the Angel Moroni, Heber once called Golden very early one morning to ask a favor. He said a reporter from *The New York Times* was on the line wanting to ask about a rumor going around the eastern seaboard. Heber was busy, and, could Golden please handle this?

The Church back then was an endless source of fascination for the eastern press, which hadn't yet come up with the idea for Elvis sightings or first-hand accounts of alien abductions.

Golden wasn't happy about the earliness of the call or what it likely portended, but he agreed to field the newspaperman's queries.

The reporter came on the line. He gave his name and said he had it on good authority that when the Second Coming was imminent, the Mormons in Salt Lake would be the first to know. The Angel Moroni on top of the Salt Lake Temple, he said, would blow his golden horn. Everyone in Utah would then know to get ready for the Lord to arrive.

Was there any truth to this story?

Golden looked at the receiver as though he hadn't heard correctly. He jabbed his finger in his ear to screw out any wax that might be lurking there. He asked the man to repeat what he'd said—something about the Second Coming and a statue and a horn?

The reporter obliged, and Golden realized that he *had* heard correctly the first time.

"There's no damn truth to it at all!" he sputtered. "If the Angel Moroni were to toot his horn, it would blow pigeon sh-- all over every one and every thing east of the temple block, *and that would never do!*"

And he slammed the phone down on the startled newsman.

Non-Returnable

The next story was told to me by a member of the Grant family. He heard it from President Grant himself.

Golden had been called in to see President Grant; something that happened far too often for Golden's taste. These interviews made him feel like a boy called to the principal's office. The reason for the interview was—you guessed it—Golden's swearing.

President Grant upbraided Golden, once again, for his lack of decorum. He was undermining the dignity of his office. As a General Authority, Golden was held to a higher standard than other Church members. Could he please reign in his incautious remarks?

It was a long and arduous dressing down. Golden tried to explain himself, but President Grant was having none of it.

In exasperation Golden threw his hands up and said, "I can't understand why you're so upset with me, Heber. Hell, you knew what you were getting when you got me!"

Back from Hawaii

This story is from a prominent Church member. It deals with a man by the name of Casper Fetzer.

Brother Fetzer was the head of a family of German converts. They came to Utah and made a name for themselves designing and manufacturing furniture. The finest furniture that was then produced in Utah came from the Fetzer family. In fact, Fetzer is still a name highly regarded in the furniture business.

At the end of November 1919, the first temple outside the continental United States was dedicated by Heber J. Grant in the Hawaiian Islands. After the dedication, President Grant returned to Salt Lake City with something on his mind.

He asked his secretary to call Brother Fetzer in. Fetzer had designed and built all of the furniture in the new temple. When he arrived, President Grant began:

"We have a problem."

"It's the U-shaped chairs in the Hawaiian Temple. You should have measured the, uh, posteriors of the sisters in Hawaii before building those chairs. A number of times I saw women get wedged in—tight!—they actually lifted your chairs with their, uh, posteriors when they stood up."

Upon hearing news of the furniture fiasco, Golden confided to a friend, "I've made plenty of blunders in my life, but never one that big. I feel for Brother Casper Fetzer. There's no way those chairs can stay in the Hawaiian Temple. All you can do is make bigger chairs. One thing is for damn sure: Nothing else is going to get any smaller."

Just a Simple Cowboy

I found a letter from Uncle Golden dated December 1, 1919. It was written to a friend, Stayner Richards.

Part of it reads, "I've been called on the carpet so many times that I've worn out a spot in front of Heber's desk. But today, Stayner, I'm grateful to be just a mule skinning cowboy and damn little else."

Sitting Poll

At a meeting dedicated to living the Word of Wisdom, President Grant gave a stirring defense of clean living. At the close of his sermon, he asked all those brethren present who were living the Word of Wisdom to please stand. He turned and said to Golden, who was seated with him on the stand, "Would you please stand and count them?"

This put Golden on the spot. His own observance of this particular commandment was notoriously lax. "No thanks, Heber; I can see them all right here from where I'm sitting."

P.D.Q. Kimball

This is a story Uncle Golden told about Heber J. Grant.

"Not so many conferences ago, I was the last one to stand and speak before the conference adjourned. President Grant told me I had seven minutes. I only took three. It was the only time President Grant ever shook my hand after one of my talks.

"And that is more than any of the Brethren had ever done."

Brethren

One of a Kind

Near the end of his life, a good friend commented: "Brother Kimball, there will never be another like you."

Uncle Golden's response was, "I'm sure that that brings a great deal of comfort to many of the Brethren."

General Observation

My Uncle Golden is sometimes called "The Swearing Apostle." That is incorrect. Golden was not an apostle; he was never called to the Council of the Twelve Apostles.

Golden was, however, in the First Quorum of Seventy, eventually becoming president when B.H. Roberts, who was the previous president of the Seventies, died in 1933. Golden presided until 1938 when he died in an automobile accident.

While technically wrong to call Golden an apostle, I have to confess "The Swearing Apostle" has a nicer ring to it than "The Swearing Seventy"—a term that conjures up that old movie, *The Dirty Dozen*. So the appelation "Swearing Apostle" fits my uncle well, if rather loosely.

Whether one is an apostle or seventy, they are all considered General Authorities—a group of high church officials collectively known as "The Brethren."

Some take Golden's comment, "I love some of the Brethren a hell of a lot more than I do others!" too literally. Some of the Brethren were clearly offended by his swearing and unvarnished spontaneity, even to the point of trying to reign him in.

The stubborn old cowboy in Golden never liked that kind of attention. But he understood that these Brethren were coming from a different perspective: "I was not raised in the same pasture as most of the other Brethren."

Not Enough Chiefs

Uncle Golden made this comment about the Brethren that I think is very insightful:

"As far as I'm concerned, there are not enough General Authorities to do all the thinking for the membership of the Church."

Getting to Know You

Most of the General Authorities absolutely thought the world of Golden. At his funeral many of them spoke, and it was clear from their comments that he was loved and appreciated.

In my lifetime I often heard President David O. McKay and President Hugh B. Brown and Elder LeGrande Richards—men who knew him—speak of him with kindness and great affection.

Golden once said, "I think I'm safer here among the Brethren that know me...although we've had a hell of a time getting acquainted, I admit."

Wind Talker

Elder Richard R. Lyman, a member of the Quorum of the Twelve Apostles, often requested either B.H. Roberts or Golden from the First Quorum of Seventy as traveling companions when he was on assignment. Golden and B.H. took turns. It was not something that either man looked forward to.

What irked them about Elder Lyman were his sermons—they were interminable; the Apostle simply didn't know when to quit.

Golden complained to his wife, Jennie, that he would cross the entire country with Brother Lyman to attend a conference, and when Brother Lyman was *finally* finished speaking there was no time left for Golden. So he was asked simply to give the closing prayer.

He told Jennie, "That's a hell of a thing. Traveling that far to give a closing prayer."

Golden decided to be candid with brother Lyman. He told him, "Richard, if you continue to take up all the time when you speak, I'm going to have to refer to you as 'Windy Dick... WINDY DICK!' Do you understand?"

This amused Richard Lyman somewhat. But the name caught on: Around Salt Lake City in some circles, "Windy Dick" became Richard Lyman's nickname.

Odd Couple

Levi Edgar Young was a fellow member of the First Quorum of Seventy. There was a great deal of mutual affection between Levi Edgar (as my uncle used to call him) and Golden.

But they were certainly an odd couple. Where Golden was very tall, Levi Edgar was very short. Where Golden was plain-spoken, Levi Edgar was loquacious.

Despite the differences, they were good friends. Such good friends, in fact, that Golden felt comfortable giving Levi Edgar a good deal of ribbing. Brother Young liked to tell this story on himself.

"I met Brother Kimball on the street and I said, 'Brother Kimball, I just want you to know what a great pleasure and privilege it is to serve with you on the First Quorum of Seventy. I also would like you to know how much I admire and esteem you and what a great source of inspiration and spiritual strength you are to me. Sir, it is an inestimable honor to serve with you!'

"Golden then said to me, 'Brother Young, I wish to hell I could say the same about you, but I can't.'"

I heard this story from Levi Edgar Young himself. After the telling, he laughed and laughed.

Small Fry

Here's another Levi Edgar Young story related to me by Sterling McMurrin.

Sterling and his mother went down to the old Church Administration Building at 47 E. South Temple to have lunch with his father, Joseph W. McMurrin, who was a member of First Quorum of Seventy. They went to McMurrin's office but couldn't find him.

They wandered around the halls and ran into Uncle Golden. "Have you seen Brother McMurrin?" Sister McMurrin asked.

"Yes, I saw him. He was in with Levi Edgar Young a minute ago." Golden indicated the way with a thumb over his shoulder.

"Maybe you ought to go and check in the little shrimp's office."

You Deserve a Break Today

This last Levi Edgar Young story was told to me by Pat Bagley, cartoonist for *The Salt Lake Tribune* (and, incidentally, the illustrator for these stories). Mr. Bagley heard it from his grandfather, Frank Bailey, who was the long-time bishop of the East Millcreek Ward. However, at the time of the story, Brother Bailey was president of the High Priest's Quorum.

Attendance had dropped off among the stake's high priests. The meeting was held rather early on Sunday morning. Some of the brothers loved their pillows a tad too much and habitually arrived late or not at all. Brother Bailey hit on a sure-fire way to get the hooky-playing high priests out, if only for one meeting: invite J. Golden Kimball to speak.

Brother Bailey was a casual acquaintance of Golden's, so he felt he had a foot in the door. He went into town and found Golden in the old church offices with Levi Edgar Young. When the invitation was delivered, Golden said, "Hell, Frank, you don't want an old reprobate like me. You want someone like Levi Edgar here. He'll give your quorum a good talk."

While Levi Edgar was a good man and fine speaker, it was noised around town that he was cowed by his strong-minded wife, a physically intimidating woman even if one wasn't five-foot-four. Brother Bailey wanted Golden, but was happy with any General Authority willing to come speak.

In the end, they both went.

For the first time in ages, the Sunday high priest meeting was packed. Golden rose to speak...Brother Young sat behind him on the podium.

"Brethren," he began, "I understand a number of you find it difficult to come to priesthood meeting on Sunday mornings. Hell, if you all had wives like Brother Young and I, you'd jump at the chance!"

Fair Warning

Many prominent men in the Church had memorable encounters with Golden Kimball. These stories were passed down and kept alive as family traditions long after these brethren passed away. Members of their families or friends of these brethren have told me a number of these stories.

Senator Reed Smoot had the distinction of being the only man in the history of the Mormon Church who was not only a United States senator but also a member of the Quorum of the Twelve Apostles.

Before Brother Smoot was called to the Twelve, he and Golden always enjoyed friendly bouts of verbal sparring. Sometimes it was politics. Sometimes it was religion.

Then Senator Smoot was called to the Quorum of Twelve Apostles.

Soon after, Golden ran into him and said, "Reed, if I'd been on better speaking terms with the Lord I would have warned him about you."

Sharp Contrast

Shortly before Uncle Golden's death, several men were chosen and ordained as assistants to the Twelve. A friend asked him what he thought about this turn of events.

He said, "It's a good idea to have some spares in the Quorum—heaven knows, there are some on it who are flats."

Don't Bank On It

Orville Adams was a very prominent civic leader in Utah for many years. He was president of Zions Bank, which the Church owned, and his offices were in that small white bank on First South and Main Street. (It's still there today. In fact, it's an historic landmark along with the big waterclock out in front.)

It was the midst of the Great Depression. Golden was on his way to the Grub-e-teria (a downtown eatery), and he passed the bank. Orville Adams came out of the bank and stopped him. "Golden, may I speak to you for just a minute.

"I've been wanting to bring this to your attention. I think you're good for the membership and they love to hear you. But you have to watch your tongue. I want to continue to hear you speak at conference, but I'm telling you, Golden, if you don't stop your swearing, I have it on good authority that the Brethren are not going to let you speak anymore.

"My advice to you," Orville continued, "is to give up your swearing. Let yourself continue to be heard. We would miss you. Will you take my advice?"

Golden looked at the banker askance and said, "Orville, I don't believe in times like these bankers should be giving advice to anyone."

Sheer Cussedness

Here's another delightful tale involving one of the Brethren.

Rudger Clawson and Golden were sent to California on assignment. This was always a source of much bemusement around Church headquarters. It would be hard to find another two men in the Church with such different temperments and sensibilities. Elder Clawson was a grimly serious fellow: think Calvin Coolidge with a testimony.

Rumor had it Rudger requested these joint engagements to reign in Golden and keep him under control.

Aunt Jennie pleaded with Golden to refrain from any swearing or getting out of control on this trip because it was so hard on

Brother Clawson. Golden said he would do the best he could.

They went to Sacramento and everything went fine—for a while.

There were two stake conferences scheduled for that weekend. Golden did well at the first conference—most of it, anyway.

In the last meeting of that first conference Golden got carried away. He had looked at the tithing records and the statistics on attendance at priesthood and sacrament meeting: The Saints weren't living up to their commitments.

He told them they were all going to hell.

When the meeting was over, Brother Clawson got up and walked out. Caught in a press of members, Golden just caught a glimpse of him leaving out of the corner of his eye. He excused himself and hurried back to the hotel to find Brother Clawson in the room, packing.

"What are you doing, Rudger? Where are you going?"

Brother Clawson said, "I just can't take it anymore. I'm going back to Salt Lake. You'll have to finish this second conference by yourself. Your swearing is just too much for me. It offends me. I can see that you're never going to change and I've had it!"

Golden didn't know what to do. So he helped him pack.

They walked out of the hotel and down to the train station. They stood there on the platform in an uncomfortable silence waiting for the train. Finally, they could see the train for Salt Lake coming. Golden thought he should say something. "Rudger, I'm sorry about this. It's just that I get worked up and I lose control and all my cowboy language comes back. I just say what's in my heart. I apologize to you."

"But Rudger, if I didn't put some 'hells' and 'damns' in my talks they wouldn't listen to me anymore than they now listen to you!"

There was a pause. Brother Clawson then threw his head back and laughed.

"Oh, Golden, you'll be the death of me. C'mon, let's finish the next conference." And they walked back to the hotel.

Live Long and Prosper

This is one of the more delightful stories that I've heard. It has Uncle Golden in his home ward in Salt Lake. His house was northeast of the Temple, almost across the street from where the new Church Conference Center stands.

A good brother told me that his grandfather lived in the same ward—the old Eighteenth—with Uncle Golden. The Eighteenth Wardhouse used to be on Second Avenue and A Street. It was moved some years ago. The brick was too far gone so they took the benches, pulpits, doors, windows, and steeple and reconstructed it on the state capitol grounds. You can see it today, though it's now called the White Chapel.

At that time, however, it was close to town where many of the Brethren lived and was their home ward. As Golden grew older he showed up with more regularity. Traveling assignments became rare due to his declining health.

Anyway, this man said his grandfather was a Gospel Doctrine teacher in the Eighteenth Ward. One Sunday he was talking about repentance and the process of repentance; how important it is that we forgive others and don't bear grudges. The Gospel Doctrine teacher was warming up to the subject when Uncle Golden came in and shuffled quietly into the back row.

"You saints here—how many of you still have enemies? How many of you still have anger in your hearts? How many of you can't forgive someone who has wronged you?"

The teacher let that sink in, then asked, "Now, by a show of hands: How many of you still have more than twenty enemies?"

A few hands went up.

"How many of you still have more than ten enemies?"

Many more hands were raised this time.

"How many of you have five enemies?"

More hands.

Then he asked this very pointed question: "How many of you
have no enemies at all?" There was a pause, then one hand went
up—Uncle Golden's.

This wasn't anticipated in the lesson plan, but the brother
forged bravely ahead. "Brother Kimball, that's wonderful. If
anyone knows about forgiveness, compassion, and true Christ-
like charity, it would be you—a man who's served the Church
for a lifetime as a General Authority."

The brother humbly asked, "Would you please come to the
front of the class and tell us how you're able to come to this
point in life without any enemies?"

Golden reluctantly shuffled up to the front of the class. "Well,
brothers and sisters, I want you to know something: I'm no great
example of righteousness or compassion or forgiveness...."

"I just outlived all those sons o' bitches."

Golden Words

Here to Eternity

Brother Kimball, why don't you come to Logan and see us anymore?" President Romney of the Utah State Agricultural College once asked.

"Ah, hell, I've preached them all into the Celestial Kingdom enough times," Golden replied. "Now they can just go to hell if they want to."

Swear Lake

Golden said his swearing was an art form he learned from the saddle in Bear Lake. Swearing was simply some of the leftovers from his cowboy days.

He tried very hard to clean up his language. He assured people that what he was left with had come from a far, far larger vocabulary.

Chicken Feed

During the Great Depression of the 1930s, Golden was often asked to encourage the members of the Church to pay a full tithe.

This task took him to Orderville to speak to the community. He was concerned that the Saints were not showing much charity or compassion towards one another. He said, "This depression is going to pass. But this selfishness that you're showing is going to stay with you. Here is an opportunity to be more giving and sharing."

He then told a story about an elderly sister. He said when he heard this story it broke his heart. This sister had next to nothing—only a few chickens.

She needed supplies from town. So one day she went to the chicken coop to gather up what eggs there were. She took these dozen eggs in her apron and oh-so-carefully walked to the store.

One by one she laid them on the counter.

The grocer, who was a hard man, looked at the eggs and said, "I'll give you a penny apiece for them—that's all—a penny apiece."

Golden asked the congregation, "Can you believe that, brothers and sisters? Just a penny apiece? Brothers and sisters, that hardly pays for wear and tear on the chicken's ass'!"

Don't Get the Wrong Idea

In Salina, Golden told the members: "Tithing is a commandment of the Lord; some of you aren't doing it. That's wrong. Repent!"

"Some of you *are* doing it. You're paying a full tithe. You feel pretty good about things. But you may be doing it with the wrong intent: Anyone who pays tithing with the idea it will bring financial reward is crazy as hell."

Spinning a Golden Yarn

On one particular occasion, Golden was asked to take a look at the Church owned woolen mills for the First Presidency. He said he'd be happy to.

He was shown around the mill by the manager. There was a great deal of noise and clatter from the machinery as it deftly wove spools of wool thread into cloth.

It was winter and Golden was wearing a frock coat. He was discussing details of the operation when his coat accidentally caught in one of the machines. It began to pull. At first he was forced to run, and then it yanked him off his feet. The spinning machinery dragged him around and around.

After several revolutions the coat broke loose, and Uncle Golden was thrown free. The manager ran up and said, "Brother Kimball! Brother Kimball! Are you all right? Speak to me!"

Uncle Golden looked up and weakly said, "I don't know why the hell I should. I passed by you several times and not once did you speak to me."

The manager took off his coat and put it underneath Uncle Golden's head. "Are you comfortable?" he asked.

Golden stopped moaning for a moment, and said, "I make a living."

Ten Percent

There was a very interesting relationship that existed in old Salt Lake between my Uncle Golden and John F. Fitzpatrick, the publisher of *The Salt Lake Tribune*. Fitzpatrick was a good Catholic who occupied his position from 1924 to 1960. The two men had a unique bond.

Jack Gallivan, who himself later became publisher of the

Tribune, has told me a number of stories that he remembers about the two. It was his responsibility once a month to go up to the Church Administration Building in a car and pick up Uncle Golden. He would then bring him back to The Salt Lake Tribune Building and escort him to the executive offices on the top floor. Uncle Golden and John F. Fitzpatrick would sit down and have lunch together.

Mr. Gallivan remembers sitting in the outer offices and listening to the two of them them swap stories and laugh about certain people or problems of the day.

On one occassion, they fell to talking about tithing in the LDS Church. Mr. Fitzpatrick understood that Golden was having to struggle with his finances and kidded Uncle Golden a bit about the tithing issue. "Come on, Golden, I know how much you're struggling. You can't possibly be paying a full ten percent tithing. You don't make enough money to enjoy the luxury of a ten percent tithing."

"You may be right, John—It is hard to pay ten percent," Golden admitted.

There was a thoughtful silence. Then Golden said, "Hell, I don't *make* ten percent!"

Nosey Newsman

On another occasion, Jack Gallivan remembers lunch was interrupted by a phone call from the Church. A Church secretary said there was a writer from *The New York Times* that wanted to talk to Brother Kimball.

The secretary apologized, but thought that perhaps the call was important. She had guessed that Uncle Golden was dining at the Tribune and would Mr. Fitzpatrick mind terribly if he turned the phone over to President Kimball?

Mr. Gallivan says he could hear what was said on Golden's end clearly. He soon gathered from the flow of the conversation that the reporter from New York was inquiring about Golden's late father and venerated church leader, Heber C. Kimball.

Was it true that Heber Kimball had forty-three wives? Did he really have forty-six sons and twenty-two daughters? Is it true there were that many children? And, in particular, were there really that many sons? As one of those sons, could Golden comment on the size of the family and would he care to verify the numbers?

Golden finally interrupted the man and said, "That's true, that's true—it was a mighty big family. I was one of forty-six sons. And do you know what?...."

"There wasn't a bastard among them!" And Golden slammed the phone down.

Mixed Nuts

On another occasion Golden stood before a congregation made up primarily of bishops and Melchizedek priesthood leaders: The men charged with keeping the Church functioning on a grass roots level.

He started by observing that "there are a great many nuts in the Church, brethren. I've observed over the years how fast and testimony meeting has become their day."

"Now, bishops, we can solve this problem. Let them speak once in a while in sacrament meeting. But feel free to tell them when they've said enough. Otherwise, it may well never damn cross their minds."

Golden Angel

Last summer in southern Utah, I did a J. Golden Kimball program for the park service at Capitol Reef. A gentleman approached me afterwards. He was an authentic American cowboy from Loa, a lovely little town not too far from the park. This cowboy was a short, bow-legged man with weather-beaten skin who spoke with a southern Utah twang. He was probably in his eighties. As he walked me back to the car, he told me this memorable story about Uncle Golden.

When he was young—a teacher in the Aaronic priesthood— he and the other boys always got a real kick out of listening to a certain man in the ward. He would stand up in fast and testimony meeting and tell about visitations he had from various people on the other side.

These were famous people: Napoleon, Lincoln, or Julius Caesar. The man's ramblings seemed innocent enough. Just like clockwork, the first Sunday of every month the man would rise and tell the ward who among the celebrated dead he'd most recently talked to. It was one of the few things that made long fast and testimony meetings bearable for young boys. In fact, they started to look forward to it.

But one Sunday, this gentleman got up and told his fellow Saints about a visitation he'd had from a golden angel. This golden angel was now appearing to him every alternating Thursday with important news: The Brethren were in apostacy;

the Church leaders were not inspired by the Lord but by the devil; they were using tithing money for their own personal gain; and they were practicing polygamy again. They were drinking coffee and liquor, and they were smoking.

The bishop was not amused. These were no longer addled ramblings from a harmless soul. He called the brother in and said, "I'm very concerned about this. You need to go to Salt Lake and talk to somebody there—a General Authority—tell him about these visitations and tell him that I had recommended you come up there."

This good brother meant no evil. He was simply passing on the message from the golden angel. He went to Salt Lake City as instructed and found the Church Administration Building. He asked to see a General Authority.

The receptionist asked what the visit was about. The man said he had been receiving revelations from a golden angel.

This receptionist was unusually astute. She said, "Oh, I'll put you in to see Brother Golden Kimball. Brother Kimball loves these kinds of things. I think that you would find it worth your while to tell him the complete story."

The man was directed to Golden's office on the second floor. Golden let the man in and said, "What can I do for you, brother?"

The man told his story about the golden angel and how the Church and General Authorities had fallen away.

The receptionist was correct; this was right up Golden's alley. "How often do you receive these visitations?"

"Every alternating Thursday. Today's Monday so he'll be visiting me this Thursday."

Uncle Golden said, "Well, so that's when...Listen, I want you to pass on some advice from me to this golden angel the next time you see him. Would you do that for me?"

The brother said yes.

"You write this down so you get it just like I tell you." The brother was handed a pencil and piece of paper. "When he appears to you on Thursday, you tell that golden angel to kiss my pink ass. There, did you get all that?"

The brother dutifully scratched away and promised to deliver the message.

The very next fast and testimony meeting this unusual brother said he'd had another visit from the golden angel. He said that he had followed Brother Kimball's directions explicitly and told the golden angel to kiss J. Golden Kimball's derriere.

That was the last visitation he received from the golden angel. In fact, it was the last visitation he received from anyone.

At the BYU

This next story was passed on to me by the Cummings family, Dick Cummings in particular.

He said his uncle, Dr. B. F. Cummings III, was on the BYU faculty. He was head of the department of foreign languages. Dr. Cummings was a good friend of Golden's.

In 1928, Golden was asked to speak at the Brigham Young University graduation commencement. Golden felt this was a great honor.

He drove to Provo on the appointed day, preparing a few thoughts before arriving. Once there he was met by a university official who ushered him through all of the preliminaries: introductions, donning the faculty robes, and marching out to the stand.

Dr. Cummings was next to Golden. As they were approaching the rostrum, Dr. Cummings turned to him and said, "Brother Kimball, this is a university. You can say anything you want: there's intellectual freedom here."

Golden threw a dubious glance at the professor. "Well, B.F., if I can say anything I want to here, it's the only damn place on God's earth that I can!"

Old College Try

It's reported that Golden gave a memorable address to the graduates at Brigham Young University. At least part of what he said has made it down to our time.

"You've finished four years of college and you think you've received a pretty decent education. You think you've learned a lot from your studies and your books. Allow an old man to pass on to you some additional wisdom gained through a lifetime of learning....

"You don't know a damn thing."

Sisteren

Sinfully Good

It was in Salina, I understand, where this story took place. There had been a fast and testimony meeting combined with a full day of conference sessions. These long fasts were hard on Uncle Golden. He was very thin to begin with, and though he didn't eat a lot, he needed a little sustenance on a regular basis. He was feeling light-headed by noon. But the meetings went over time and it wasn't until late in the afternoon that they finally had a break.

Golden was to dine with the stake president and his family. On the way to the stake president's home, Golden's unhappy thought was that now he'd have to wait another hour or so for the meal to be prepared.

To his surprise, the stake president's wife, a woman named Olive McKeen, had skipped out on some of the later meetings to come home early. When they arrived, the meal was on the table. The plates were out, the water was in the glasses, and the roast beef and mashed potatoes were ready to eat.

Golden came into the dining room with the table groaning under the load of so much succulent food. He blinked in surprise.

Looking at Sister McKeen with tears of gratitude welling up in his eyes, he said, "Oh Olive, I just love ya—I could break all of the Ten Commandments with you for doing this!"

Let Them Eat Cake

On the subject of food, there are a couple of stories that have come to my attention. Sister Widtsoe, the wife of Elder John Widtsoe, had quite a reputation for championing the virtues of natural foods and a strict adherence to the Word of Wisdom.

Using the eighty-ninth section of the Doctrine and Covenants as her guiding source, she drew up a list of foods that one should refrain from eating.

She gave this list to Golden Kimball one day and asked him to look it over. She then hinted that a man of God would alter his diet accordingly.

Uncle Golden looked down the list at all the foods that he shouldn't be eating. After finally arriving at the bottom of the exhaustive and detailed list, he said, "Good hell, chocolate cake will go next!"

Too Much of a Chaste Thing

As a member of the First Quorum of Seventy, Golden was required to do a lot of traveling. One assignment had him addressing a room full of the fairer sex at a young women's conference in northern Idaho.

"I want to say a few words to you young sisters about sinning...," he began.

"Don't do it!"

"It's not good. Keep it out of your life! I want you to keep your virtue. And when you find a good worthy man to take you to the temple, you want to be able to tell your bishop you're as pure as the snow and you've never drifted." The sisters chuckled appreciatively at this play on words. But Golden wasn't finished.

"I want to pass on some more advice to you sisters. It doesn't end there. I would strongly encourage you to commit yourselves to abstinence before you marry rather than *after* you marry."

Uncle Golden was to say later that what few men were in the meeting went out of the way to thank him for his remarks.

Little Stream

After a meeting in Kanosh, a woman came up to Uncle Golden and said she was tired of General Authorities coming down to central Utah and telling everyone how to live their lives. She said, "We have the Bible; all we need is the Lord. All we have to do is follow His example. He is all powerful."

She went on to say that "He made the grass green, He made the sky blue, and He made the waters to flow...."

Golden, who was getting on in years, stopped her right there. "Well, sister," he said, "you may be right about making the grass green. And you're also probably right about how He makes the skies blue. But I need to take issue with you on making the waters flow."

SURE,
I'LL MARRY
YOU...

Tough Love

Golden was asked to speak to a chapel full of single men in Utah County one evening. He decided to give them some good, honest advice about marriage.

"I would counsel you single brethren to marry a girl from Sanpete County.

"With these young sisters, it does not matter how bad things may get in your married lives. Crop failure, pestilence, famine, drought, financial crisis, bad teeth, or poor health; it won't faze them.

"Just keep in mind that despite what a poor prospect you might be, these young sisters have experienced far, far worse. They'll stick with you brethren."

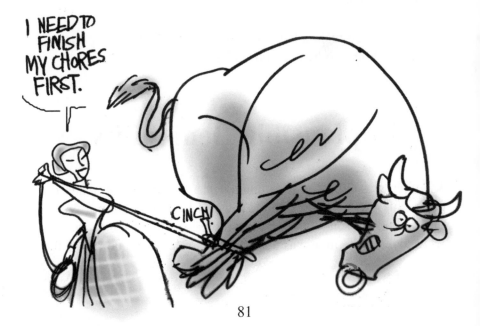

81

Twofer

Golden shared this story about his father, Heber C. Kimball, with an intimate group of friends.

"My father told a congregation of women who were still single to find a man they wanted and go up and tell him of the desires of their heart. Well, twin sisters came up to my father after the meeting and asked, 'Did you mean what you said?' My father said, 'Yes I did.'

"One of the twins said, 'Brother Kimball, I want to marry you. But so does my sister. Between the two of us we can't decide who it should be, so you'll have to choose between me and my sister.'"

"What did your father do?" someone asked.

"Oh," Golden responded, "he didn't want to hurt either one of their feelings, so he married both of them."

Implausible Deniability

Golden was called on to attend a hearing of a brother accused of a sexual transgression. In the town of Logan, the rumor was that he and the school marm were more than just friends; they were lovers. The man was a sheepherder. He would come off the mountain and park his sheep trailer and horses right in front of the woman's house for weeks at a time.

The local priesthood authorities called for a hearing and an investigation. They also asked Uncle Golden, who at this time was a General Authority, to sit in. He obliged and traveled into town from his ranch.

The sheepherder was present, offering up an unconvincing explanation for his suspicious activities. The priesthood leaders carefully questioned him about his moral worthiness. He flatly denied doing anything wrong.

What was he doing parking his wagon and sheep trailer in front of her house? "Oh, we're just friends. But I didn't do that thing that you accuse me of."

He was seen coming and going from the house at all hours. "Well, the sister is alone and sometimes I go over to help out and fix things. But I didn't do that thing that you accuse me of."

He'd been observed entering the house late and staying all night long. "Well, you see, occasionally I fall asleep there and sleep on the couch. But I didn't do that thing that you accuse me of."

Did he ever go into the bedroom? "Sometimes I did. If she was lonely or cold, well, sure—sometimes I would get in bed with her. But I didn't do that thing that you accuse me of!"

The local church leaders asked the man to step outside so they could consider the matter amongst themselves.

The brethren mulled over the man's answers. Despite his stout denials of ever having had sex with that woman, the leaders were leaning towards excommunication. How likely was it that they could have slept together but not "slept together?"

They asked Golden for his thoughts. He'd been quiet up to this point. He cleared his throat and said, "Brethren, I think we ought to excommunicate the son of a bitch."

"But, Brother Kimball—the man denies doing anything that merits excommunication. He says he never had sexual intercourse with the sister."

"Well, if he didn't, then he obviously doesn't have the blood of Israel in him!"

Hush Little Baby

On a hot afternoon in Mesa, Arizona, Uncle Golden was attempting to address an audience that was filled with crying babies. He finally stopped.

"I can't hear the Spirit speak to me because of all this damn racket! It's either these children or me. Now which do you want to hear. Do you want to hear me? Raise your hands if you do."

The audience raised its hands.

"Or do you want to hear these damn children cry? Raise your hands."

Nobody raised their hand.

"It looks like I won the vote."

Having handily won the plebiscite against cranky chidren, Golden relented a little. "Now, you sisters take your children outside and while you're there, give them a little nourishment and change their diapers. It will work wonders for everyone's disposition."

"Particularly mine."

What's Up, Doc?

Another story came to me from a Sister Elizabeth Smith. She said her uncle, Ben Johnson, was a medical doctor. He was Golden's doctor and was more than happy to see the old man whenever he needed medical attention.

Dr. Johnson billed Golden modestly for his services. The real payoff for the doctor was the opportunity to chat with Golden about this and that. They would talk and laugh for hours.

Doctor Johnson once complained to Golden about a woman who came to see him far too often. He told Uncle Golden he'd taken out her adenoids, her appendix, her tonsils, and still she wanted the attention of a good doctor. She wanted just about everything removed that could be removed.

Golden suddenly brightened. "Hell, Ben, I know what you should do—just take out her belly button and put in a zipper."

Horse Sense

Last summer I was asked to present my J. Golden Kimball program in Cedar City, Utah, to help raise money for a new library. I gave my usual presentation, and we had a pretty good crowd.

When the evening was over a woman came up and told me the following story:

"I had a great aunt who was a tremendous admirer of your uncle. She never married. She got by fairly well, though. A ranch had been left to her on the outskirts of Cedar City. She was the only heir to the estate. Rather than sell out and move into town, she chose to run that ranch on her own.

"It was a big ranch with lots of horses. She had a great love for all of her horses. There was one in particular—a quarter horse that was her very favorite.

"When she heard that Golden Kimball was coming to speak at the tabernacle in St. George, she rode that horse all the way down from Cedar City. She had an important question for Brother Kimball. It was about her horse.

"When the conference was over she waited outside for him. He came out and was surrounded by people. It took him a moment, but Golden saw her patiently waiting, and he excused himself. He walked over and asked if there was something he could do for her. She said, 'Brother Kimball, I've been waiting to talk to you for a long time.'

"Golden said, 'I could see you wanted to talk to me. And I could see by the look on your face that something is troubling you. How can I help you, sister?'

"'Well, Brother Kimball,' she said, 'I have never married. I had the responsibility of a ranch with a lot of horses and cattle and I dedicated my life to that.' My great aunt pointed towards her horse. 'See that horse over there? That's my horse. That's my favorite. Now, I have kind of a peculiar question to ask you, Brother Kimball.'

"I'm sure Brother Kimball had been asked lots of peculiar questions in his life. Nevertheless, he seemed genuinely curious about what my old rancher-aunt wanted to know.'

"'I don't wish to sound irreverent,' she continued, 'but I really want to know: Will I see that horse on the other side? Will I see him in heaven?'

"Brother Kimball looked at the horse and looked at my great aunt. She noted he had a twinkle in his eye when he said, 'Sister, there are a lot of horse's asses in the Church that think they're going to heaven. Why not the rest of your horse?'"

The South

Golden Gunflinger

I worked in Jackson, Mississippi, the summer of 1959 as a writer for a paper called *The Jackson State Times*. I wrote a column which, I believe, contributed to the demise of the newspaper. Whatever the reason, it had to close down, and I moved back home to Utah in the fall of that year.

The whole painful experience was worthwhile, however, because of a man I met at church in Mississippi and the story he told me.

It happened years ago in the backwoods of Arkansas. The man's grandfather remembered when Golden was president of the Southern States Mission. This would have been 1892 or '93.

He said that Uncle Golden traveled to Arkansas to attend a meeting of the Saints. This meeting was to be held in an old abandoned Baptist church that the members had rented. For several months it served as a place where they could hold their services and hear church leaders speak when they were in the area.

When Golden arrived late that day, he encountered a mob surrounding this old Baptist church. The raucous members of the mob weren't going to let the "accursed Mormons" into the building. The members were sitting on the perimeter of the mob in their wagons waiting for Golden to arrive.

He rode up, dismounted, and tied his horse up to a hitching

post. He sized up the situation for a moment. Then, telling the members to follow him, he walked straight through the mob toward the front of the meeting house. At the door several men blocked his entry. They were all armed to the teeth: pistols in their hands and knives stuck in their belts.

Golden looked them straight in the face and said, "I'm here to preach the Gospel of Jesus Christ to my fellow Saints. We have rented this church for that purpose. Now get the hell out of the way."

He pushed through the ruffians and went into the meeting house, the members in tow.

The man relating the story was a teenager at the time. He remembered it all vividly and swore to the truth of what happened next. Golden said a prayer and began to preach a sermon from the pulpit. He hadn't gone very far when a vol-ley of gunfire destroyed the chapel's front door—some of the bullets lodged in the pulpit itself.

FETCH!

Golden stopped talking, left the pulpit, marched down the center aisle, and kicked the remains of the door out of his way. He grabbed the mob leader's smoking gun out of his hand and threw it off into the woods. He then wheeled on the startled man. "You keep that up, you son of a bitch, and you're going to kill some of these innocent people here. Now go and find your gun and all of you go home and tell your wives what brave bastards you were tonight to come out here and put fear in these people's hearts!"

Golden marched back in to continue his sermon. Members of the mob began drifting off, one supposes to go home. What they told their wives isn't known.

Howling Bad Time

Here's another story from the time that Golden was president of the Southern States Mission. It involves an elder whose name was Willard Bean. He was quite a colorful man himself. Dubbed the "Fighting Pastor," he had been a prize fighter before going in the mission field.

Golden attended a mission conference in the city of Mine Lick, Tennessee, in 1892. As mission president, Golden was there to preside.

The missionaries of the Central Tennessee District decided at the last moment that they would present a hymn at this conference. By their own admission, their presentation of this hymn, unfortunately, rang both high and loud in certain parts.

Golden arrived and heard the elders practicing—in fact it was impossible not to. He stood there for several minutes listening. He then asked Elder Willard Bean, who was leading the singing, to step outside with him.

When they got outside, he said, "Now, Elder Bean, I think it best that we have you and the other missionaries sing in another room. We'll bore some holes in the door and let a little in at a time. You see, my eardrums can't take it all at once."

He said later their singing was the damnedest disturbance he'd ever heard in his whole life. Bean good naturedly recorded all this in his diary and passed it on.

Pointy Headed KKKooks

The Klu Klux Klan was an organization that Golden had the greatest contempt for. He personally witnessed their inhumanity against Blacks, Jews, and (on a first-hand basis) Mormons. He thought they were imbeciles of the highest order.

Golden had many encounters with the Klan, both as missionary and mission president. His disdain for the men in sheets made him reckless. In every encounter, he wouldn't let them have the upper hand.

Mormon missionaries were accused by the Klan of seducing the wives and daughters of the White South to be taken back to live in polygamous slavery in Utah. Golden said one only had to look at their wives and daughters to know that such a thing couldn't possibly be true. Even polygamists have standards.

In a letter home, he said this of the Klan: "It's a waste of a good sheet."

He described to his brother Elias how the Klan dressed. "They cover themselves in a white sheet and there's a hood for the head with two small openings for their eyes. This hood has a point to it, which is more than could be said for their beliefs."

Tea Teaser

During his years in the Southern States Mission, Golden never let the Klan stop him; that job fell to a mosquito.

He picked up malaria as a missionary and it continued with him for years. Sometimes he would be laid low by a recurrence of the fever and chills. On more than one occasion he was bed ridden for weeks.

In 1891, he records an incident that occured in Chattonooga, Tennessee.

While suffering from another bout of malaria, he was confined to a bed in the home of a convert family. They had been very kind to him and put him in a darkened room upstairs. The wife brought him food when he could take it and attended to his fevers.

One day she quietly tapped on the door and came in. She was carrying a cup and teapot. "Brother Kimball," she meekly began, "I prepared this weak tea for you. I think if you try it you'll feel better. I hope that doesn't offend you."

Golden leaned up in the bed and said, "Sister, if I'm going to break the Word of Wisdom, let's make it full strength."

All Meetinged Out

In April of 1892, Golden was made a member of the First Quorum of Seventy. He was still serving in the Southern States Mission as president, so for a short while he wore two hats. He was eventually replaced by his brother, Elias.

In the meantime he attended a number of meetings as a member of the First Quorum of Seventy. On one occassion he had been attending several meetings in the Cincinnati area. It had been a long day. It was fast Sunday and the meeting had gone on from early in the morning until late in the afternoon. It was a grumpy Golden that left the church.

He went to a member's home for a small bite to eat. The leading Church authority in the Cincinnati area, however, reminded Golden there was one more meeting they had yet to attend.

Golden was exhausted. "Do we really have to attend this meeting?"

This leader said, "Yes, we do: It's going to be a good meeting."

Golden snapped, "It better be a damn good meeting to be better than no meeting at all!"

Watch and Pray

While on his mission, Golden was paired with an Elder Welch in northern Georgia. They preached the Gospel without "purse nor script," meaning they relied on the charity of the locals for food and lodging. Most of the time this worked....

They wandered back roads into the Georgia hollows and woods looking for signs of habitation. If they were lucky, they found interested listeners, a simple meal, and a place to sleep. Even if it was only a barn.

The homesteads became fewer and fewer and the woods grew thicker and thicker. It dawned on them after a few days of wandering blind without encountering a soul that they were lost.

They were scared, hungry, and without a clue as to where to go next. Golden recommended that they get on their knees and pray for the Spirit to show them the way out. Elder Welch offered the prayer. It was a long prayer. It went on and on.

And on.

Elder Welch was using every "thine, "thee," "thou," and "thy" in the book with a smattering of "willst's" and "doest's" for good measure. He called for blessings on the poor and destitute and meek and widows and orphans and needy and leaders of the Church until Golden thought it was never going to end.

Finally, he got to the most important part: "Wouldst Thou, oh Lord, find it meet in Thy grand design to show us, Thine humble servants, the way that we might tread to find our way back home?" And then they said, "Amen."

When they looked up there were men with rifles approaching on horseback. Luckily, it was dark. Golden and Welch got up and "we ran like hell." The horsemen took a few shots but didn't hit the fleeing elders.

They soon found their way out and arrived back where they started.

This experience made such an impression on Golden that for a long time after he said he "prayed with one eye open."

The Golden Touch

Generally Speaking

Near the end of his life, Golden was discussing the principal of revelation with a friend.

He reflected back on his reckless cowboy days and said, "When the Lord calls an old cowboy-muleskinner like me to be a General Authority, brother, I tell you it has to be revelation."

Running Late

Many stories have come to my attention over the past few years that are illustrative of the love that Uncle Golden felt for the average Latter-day Saint. Golden had tremendous empathy for the downtrodden and afflicted.

A lovely woman by the name of Wendy told me that she had an older sister that suffered from multiple sclerosis. The sister, who was confined to a wheelchair, lived about a block from Temple Square.

Wendy tells the story: "On beautiful summer days I would try to find a few hours to go see my sister and take her for a walk. I would push her in her wheelchair down to the gardens west of the old Church administrative offices and then on over to Temple Square.

"On one of those days we were going around looking at the flowers and taking in the beauty of that spot. Way off in the distance my sister saw someone. 'Isn't that Brother Golden Kimball running across that main thoroughfare in the middle of the block?' she asked.

"I looked, and sure enough, it was him. I said, 'That's Brother Kimball and he sure looks like he's in a big hurry. It's Thursday, perhaps it's the weekly meeting in the Temple of the Brethren and he's late.'

"My sister said, 'Oh, Wendy, would you please try and catch him? I'd just love to shake his hand! I've always admired and loved him. Please let's try. We can catch him! Please will you?'

"So I said, 'Okay, but you hang on!' and off we went in hot pursuit. We were racing to try and intercept him and were yelling 'Brother Kimball! Brother Kimball!' But he was way ahead of us.

"It looked hopeless. Then someone stopped him and pointed back to us. He turned around and looked at us. Then, as though he had all the time in the world, he walked back to us. He didn't look at me—he looked at my sister. He knelt down, took her hand, and he kissed her on the cheek. He said, 'Remember, my dear, there will yet be better times.'

"He got up, wished me a good day, and walked to the Temple. Neither of us ever forgot that experience."

Resurrection Morn

This story comes from Steve Smoot. Steve had a single aunt with a delightful sense of humor. Before she died, Steve asked her to record some of her early recollections for the family oral history.

On the tape he asked her if she remembered Golden Kimball. "Oh, yes, of course. I just loved the man. He was such a delight. He was one of my favorite General Authorities."

Steve then asked if there was any particular memory she had of him. "Yes, we all lived in the Eighteenth Ward together. Often times we would have a party and invite Brother Kimball to come along.

"If he was in town and if he was feeling well he would join us. We'd have Christmas parties, birthday parties, and Twenty-fourth of July parties. Yes, occasionally he would be there.

"I remember this one particular party. We picked up Brother Kimball and went to the party. We were all having a good time, but he was there quietly sitting in the corner.

"Somehow the conversation got around to the fact that I was the only single woman in the room. They were kidding me, but the joshing got a little mean. What was I going to do on the morning of the first resurrection with no husband? I just tried to pass it off and said, 'Oh, I'll just sleep a little longer. You all go on ahead without me and find your mates.' But they said, "You won't have a mate. What will you do when you finally awaken?'

"I was getting embarrassed. It was hard on me, but they still were at it when Brother Kimball interrupted and said, 'Let me tell you about some experiences I had when I was off on a conference assignment last weekend.' He had sensed my embarrassment and changed the whole direction of the conversation.

"He told us stories about some of the people he had met and humorous experiences he had. I was very relieved and grateful. The subject of my being single didn't come up again. Nothing more was said of it.

"We took Brother Kimball home in the car that night. I was right behind him. He was in the right hand side of the car next to the driver. We dropped him off at his home and he waved and thanked us all and started down the driveway.

"Then he turned, raised his cane and said, 'Wait a minute! Wait a minute!' He came to my side of the car and tapped on the window. I rolled the window down. He looked in at me and said, 'Irma, I want you to know something. On that morning of the first resurrection, don't you be worried—I'll be there for you.' Then he turned and walked back to the house.

"I was absolutely in tears. He was a lovely, lovely man."

Rain Man

J. Golden Kimball is said to have gone to St. George for a conference during a drought. In his sermon, in the first session, he was caught up in the spirit of the moment. Overwhelmed by the faith of the people there who had pioneered the harsh southern Utah country, he made promises of rain and a fruitful harvest to the dry-as-a-bone Dixie Mormons.

Later in the day when time for the second session rolled around, Elder Kimball could not be found. The stake president went out looking for the missing General Authority. He found Uncle Golden out in the barn banging his head on one of the timbers. He kept repeating, "I shouldn't have done it! I shouldn't have done it!"

"Done what?" the stake president asked.

"Made all those promises. There isn't one chance in hell one of them will come true!"

Golden left the conference convinced he'd made a mistake.

I think you can guess what happened: The rains came, and the harvest was very fruitful.

A Golden Choice

This came to me from Richard Turley. He sent it to me in a letter that outlined the following story.

When Henry Lunt resigned his calling as bishop in Cedar City, J. Golden Kimball was sent down to organize a new bishopric. When he arrived at the meeting, he looked over the audience very long and carefully. He scrutinized the men sitting on the south side of the chapel. (By the way, in those days the men and women sat apart.)

Finally Golden spoke, pointing to one man. "You—you with the mustache and the sandy hair. Yes, I mean you. Come up on the stand and sit here by me. You'll be the new bishop."

The congregation registered surprise that he'd chosen Will Corey but went ahead and sustained Golden's choice.

Afterwards the question was asked why in the world did he choose Brother Corey, who everybody knew wasn't active? Golden said, "Well, I know he isn't a church man, but I tell you something: I wanted a man who could kick the hell out of those people, and he looked like just the sort to do it."

That memorable answer has been passed down by the folks in Cedar City to the present day. It's become part of the fabric of the town's history. Needless to say, William H. Corey went on to become one of Cedar City's most outstanding bishops for more than twenty-five years.

Martyr

Late in his life, Uncle Golden was continually asked to speak at funerals—one of the many subtle compliments paid to him.

Funerals, however, were always a delicate assigment for Golden. His natural wit had to be reigned in on such occassions. He didn't want to say anything that was in bad taste.

But still he managed to offer some memorable zingers.

Speaking at the funeral of a friend in San Francisco, Golden made the comment, "The deceased was a good man. I knew him; he was a very good man. He read *The Deseret News*, and it takes a damn good man to read *The Deseret News*."

Ticket to Nowhere

On another occasion, he said, "I've given many a man a ticket to the Celestial glory that I knew wouldn't take him half way there."

Grave Matters

When Brother B.H. Roberts, president of First Quorum of Seventy, died in 1933, the family asked that Uncle Golden dedicate the grave.

The burial was planned to be in Centerville, Utah. The Cemetery there had fallen on hard times: lots of weeds, overgrown grass, picket fences falling down. It was a pathetic sight with headstones sticking up willy-nilly among the brambles.

Friends and family gathered around the grave for the dedication ceremony. Golden took his place at the head of the grave and looked around at the sad little cemetery.

"Before I dedicate this grave, I want to say something. This is one hell of a place to bury one of the Lord's anointed."

He then offered the dedicatory prayer.

Some of the city fathers were there, and Golden's comments shamed them into action. They appropriated money to repair the picket fence, clear out the weeds, and put in new grass. Today, the Centerville Cemetery is a place of beauty and a source of civic pride.

Oh, Brother

Golden was asked by President Grant to represent the Brethren at a graveside funeral service of a Kaysville banker who died wealthy, but without a single friend.

The deceased and his only brother had amassed a fortune loaning money to poor farmers at high interest rates and foreclosing on them for the smallest of infractions.

Only Golden, the bishop, and the overworked, underpaid secretary of the departed attended the service.

The bishop could not think of a thing to say about this man. He stumbled through a few platitudes then, in desperation, turned to Uncle Golden and asked him to offer a few words.

Caught completely off guard, Golden stepped up to the mahogany casket, paused for several moments, then commented, "His brother was worse! Amen."

Passing Thought

In St. George, a very humble lady had passed away. She'd given her life to helping others and raising a big family. She'd met a lot of trials with grace and courage. Everyone loved her.

At her funeral, Golden observed: "This fine old lady will be a hell of a lot better off on the other side than the Grants and the Cannons and the Snows."

Last Words

Just Desserts

As Uncle Golden approached his mid-eighties (usually deemed a good decade in which to consider what lies ahead) a friend put an arm around him and said, "Golden, you needn't be afraid, you'll get justice."

Golden's response was, "Yeah, that's just the very thing that has me worried."

Last Words...

My research shows that the last bit of advice Uncle Golden ever gave was to an old friend named Howard Keene.

He said, "Howard don't you get too damn good for me."

This is significant only because Uncle Golden left the next day for San Francisco to visit his daughter, Elizabeth, with Jennie, his wife. On the return journey to Salt Lake City, he was killed in an automobile accident in Nevada. The date was September 2, 1938. He was eighty-five years old.

My father attended the funeral. He said that it was a crowded affair. People from all walks of life came to pay their respects to

Uncle Golden: Catholics, Protestants, Indians, Jews, Mormons, non-Mormons.

There was a story going around the funeral...Uncle Golden abruptly arrived at the pearly gates. Saint Peter was there and said, "Well! If it isn't Brother J. Golden Kimball: We finally got you here."

And Uncle Golden said, "Hell, you had to kill me to do it!"

...And Testament

Thus ended the colorful earthly existence of my Uncle Golden. The Mormon people have never had a man like him before and may never have another again. During his long service to the Church, he touched the hearts of the rank and file of the members. He swore like they did, and they loved him for it. And then there was that wonderful wit about him. This ability to see things as they are—not as they should be—but as they are, and then describe it in his own amusing and original way.

Uncle Golden possessed an uncommon gift.

He is a unique personality in Mormon culture. Everything he ever said or did evidenced the warmth of a soul full of love and understanding. He remains a man deeply appreciated by all who knew him—and those who know of him through these stories.

About the Author

Born in LaVerkin, Utah, in 1934 Jim was raised around people who delighted in both telling and hearing Golden Kimball stories. "I began to collect these stories and trace their authenticity as a young man. The first piece that I wrote on his life was published in Sunstone Magazine in the early 1970s. After that, the requests for me to perform and take on his persona began. In the last twenty-five years, I have portrayed his life and told his stories before thousands of people.

"After almost every show, members of the audience will come up and tell me their favorite Golden Kimball story. This helps in my research on my great uncle's biography and adds to the character of the performance. This was also one of the biggest resources for the stories told in the first J. Golden Kimball book.

"I do this to keep alive the memory of an extraordinary man who was not afraid to be himself," Jim Kimball comments. "I believe Uncle Golden was largely misunderstood. Many people remember him as a swearing Mormon elder who told jokes. He never told a joke in his life. Golden only made amusing observations about the ironies of Mormon life. He had an unvarnished, spontaneous wit."

In August of 1996 KUED filmed Jim's depiction of his famous relative in a one hour presentation as part of the station's semi-annual fundraiser. The public's response was overwhelming. It exceeded KUED's most optimistic expectations and won several awards in international film and video competition for documentary and special interest programming.

In the summer of 1998 KUED filmed a second production titled *On the Road with Uncle Golden.* This program aired in December 1998 to an enthusiastic television audience.

Asked why the public's response was so spirited and receptive, Jim remarks, "I think it has to do with Uncle Golden's common touch. People remember him and love him because he genuinely made them laugh—primarily at themselves."

Jim lives in Salt Lake City with his wife, Joan, and is an adjunct professor at Salt Lake Community College. He hopes to complete the definitive work of his great uncle's life within the next year. In his spare time, he is working on a script for a Hollywood film on the life of Uncle Golden.

About the Illustrator

Besides his twenty-four year career as *The Salt Lake Tribune's* award winning political cartoonist, Pat Bagley is also an author and humorist specializing in things Mormon and Utahn. No one wields a chainsaw with more compassion than he does.

Pat's roots in the Beehive State run deep. He is a fifth generation Utahn, born in Salt Lake City but raised in Southern California. His mother taught school, and his father was mayor of a booming seaside community. He remembers well the annual pilgrimages to Utah to visit relatives: a station wagon crammed with four kids, two adults, and accompanying baggage (both physical and emotional).

He returned for good to Utah in 1977 following an LDS mission to Bolivia. He graduated from BYU in 1979 with a degree in political science and a minor in history which he put to good use by drawing caricatures in the Orem Mall for a summer.

Over the past two decades, he has published several books and produced six thousand cartoons for the editorial pages of *The Salt Lake Tribune*, many of which have won awards or found their way into publications including *Time, The Washington Post,* and *The Guardian* of London.

Pat achieved international renown by producing some of the most popular pins during the pin craze surrounding the 2002 Olympics. His "Seven Brides for One Brother" was a much sought-after classic as was the "Crickets Make Me Barf" seagull pin.

Pat's books include several LDS bestsellers which appeal to Mormons of all faiths, such as the first *J. Golden Kimball Stories, I Spy a Nephite, Norman and the A-Maze-ing Conference Center, The Book of Mormon Timeline, The Church History Timeline*, and a series of books produced with humor columnist Robert Kirby: *Sunday of the Living Dead, Wake Me for the Resurrection*, and *Family Home Screaming*.

His Utah books are also tremendously popular: *Welcome to Utah,* a book of hilarious cartoons; *This is the Place*, a children's history of Utah coauthored by his brother, historian Will Bagley; and *Dinosaurs of Utah*, coauthored with Gayen Wharton. They are all staples for anyone with an interest in the culture and history of this fascinating state.

Pat currently lives in Salt Lake City with his sons, Miles and Alec; a cat, Tiger; and their dog, Balto.

If you have any J. Golden Kimball stories that you wish to share with James Kimball, please mail them to the following address:

James Kimball
36 Dartmoor Place
Salt Lake City, Utah 84103